Terms and Conditions

Table Of Contents

Foreword

Everybody could use some surplus money, especially in hard times. Maybe the bills were a bit more than you'd anticipated this month or perhaps you're attempting to raise some starter cash for your own online startup or business or perhaps you just need to figure out how to ramp up your existing business.

Freelancers are a forward-looking lot. All the same, almost every day I get questions from those who find it difficult to make a sustainable living. I ascribe most of this to some people's inability to think differently.

There are a lot of ways to make income as a freelance person that I keep a file of thoughts. While I seldom find myself without a project on my desk, when work gets scarce, I go through this file to perk up the brain cells. Today I'll share the ideas with you.

Fast Freelancing Funds

Get Instant Work And Fast Cash With Your Skills.

Chapter 1:

Edit Sites

Synopsis

This might call for a bit of up front work, however may bring in dollars for a long time to come. There are so many web sites in painful need of great copy that all you have to do is switch on your computer to turn one up. All the same, the key is to target those who are willing to compensate for your services.

Fix It

An acquaintance of mine knows an apothecary who made a skin care product. The product is distributed across the country through independent distributors. My acquaintance told me to check over the site to see if it was a product I'd be interested in trying out.

When I got to the site, I instantly forgot about why I was supposed to be viewing the web site. How come? The grammar, artwork and layout were atrocious; particularly the grammar! I rewrote the home page and sent it off to the webmaster with a courteous note stating that I'd be happy to remake the entire site for $x. Inside a few days we came to terms and I got the job. You are able to do this also.

Professionals are a good target market for freelancers. Mortgage companies, insurance companies, lawn care suppliers, and so forth. Most have sites – and a lot of them are not very good. So, edit/re-script a page and send it to them with a proposition to do the whole web site. Commonly, if they use you once, they'll continue to do so for years to come. Offer to add each week, each month, every quarter, and etcetera. Add articles to the site to step-up traffic. A lot of small business owners are so busy that they don't think or understand how to do this type of marketing. Call attention to the advantages and watch your customer list grow.

Consider the content for each page. For instance, you are able to go into company history on the "About Us" page, but you can likewise mention that your company has x years of experience on the home page, also. You are able to bullet your services on the home page and then go into detail about them on the "Services" page. Jot down some points for the content of each page. Decide where you want particular tidbits to be highlighted so each page isn't repetitious.

Add a little SEO. Do some research on the net to determine what keywords are "red-hot" for the industry. If the company, for instance, makes kitchen cabinets, you might want to include terms like "kitchen remodeling" "kitchen cabinets" and "kitchen cabinetry" to name some. It's likewise a good idea to provide a regional aspect for individuals seeking the business locally. For instance, "kitchen cabinet maker in AZ" and "kitchen cabinets AZ" are good terms to work into the copy.

Utilize an attention-grabbing headline for each page. Rather than "Cabinet Makers" you may try something like "Distinctive Cabinets for Custom Kitchens." When you get into the "core," remember to talk to your specified audience. Will you refer to the customer directly? No one truly cares about the content unless it offers them something. Rather than bragging about why the company is the best, or presenting a history of kitchen cabinets it's beneficial to keep in mind that you need to explain the advantages of what the company has to offer. What can Joe Blow get out of the site, and why should he pick this company to build his cabinets?

I always end each page with an easy "call to action." For instance, "Are you ready to discover how you are able to have the kitchen of your dreams? Contact us at (phone) or email us at (e-mail)." You get the idea. The goal is to drive the reader to take action.

Chapter 2:

Author A Book

Synopsis

Make an e-book: all right, you're thought is – everyone and his father are doing this these days. However, why? Because it works. If you're well-educated about a certain topic, e.g., how to weather coat a deck, power wash a house, give up smoking, make doll apparel – whatever it is, author a book about it..

E-book

Authoring e-books is simple – it may be done in as little as twenty-four hours – and you can offer it for sale on a web site like Click Bank or Commission Junction. Think though, most individuals look to the net for info. And, "how to" info is among the most popular forms.

So, squeeze your brain for what you like to do, author an e-book about it and sell it through a major distributor like Click Bank. One book likely won't make you rich, but it may bring in extra cash for a long time to come. The most beneficial part about this idea, once you make one e-book, you are able to make others and truly build your income to the point where you are able to quit your awful day job.

Think about your target audience, your book's advantages to them, its core, and center like a laser on that. It might seem to you that just everybody' will want to read your book - but that idea may make your book too 'generalized'. Remember, if you center your efforts on a particular topic instead of generalizing you'll appeal powerfully to a certain audience and reap more possible sales. It's rather like centering on a puddle rather than an ocean.

Get to Understand your target readers; what troubles might your book resolve for them? Where is your book purchasing audience? Try to author a title that includes your audience in it. If not there, then maybe in the sub-title?

You have to be author and promoter, so write and make your sales info about your book as you author your book. Collect data about yourself for your author blurb (whatever qualifies you to author the book, maybe other publishing credits, any experience that's a plus), write about the advantages your potential purchasers are seeking and are likely to discover in your book. Get a few testimonials.

Check into places like Amazon to see what books are selling well and read their 'blurb' content for thoughts on how to present your own. A visit to your local bookshop is a great idea also. Check into some of the other marketers who are marketing books online. Do an 'E-book' search. How are they marketing?

Author an attention-getting table of contents for your book. Title your chapter and add a sub-title to make it transparent to your reader what is contained inside. Read the table of contents of other authors to get an approximation of what may be 'attention-getting'.

That should get you going. Now, do some net searches, hunt down the needed info to get yourself set in motion, but mind the rip-off artist out to get your money. Subscribe to a few newsletters by individuals who are legit. Think about each step of the process, keep notes and keep acting.

Chapter 3:

Slogans and Such

Synopsis

There are places like CafePress.com or zazzle.com that let you make t-shirts, mugs, stickers, etc. and sell them without carrying any stock yourself. There are no lower limits, nothing for you to stock and no upfront fees. If you don't sell anything, you don't pay anything.

Create

So, how may a freelancer make the best of this medium? Rather simply, if you're mighty with the pen, then dollars may follow. Make cool slogans and humorous sayings and put them on tee shirts, stickers, mugs, and so forth. You may be the creator of the next big fad Tee. Think of the motto, "Sh*t Happens?" I think this was made popular in the flower child seventies. Can you even start to guess how many bumper stickers and tee shirts were sold with this? So, squeeze your brain and produce some fantastic pop culture!

T-shirts come in an assortment of styles and colors. Are you targeting a female audience? You may consider one of the many tee shirts made for women--the baby doll, tank, spaghetti straps, and so forth. Consider the color of the shirt. While colors are attention-getting, they may also clash or overwhelm out one another. Make certain the colors you choose-- for the T-shirt itself, any printed message and the colors in any graphic --will work together to produce your canvas. You want your shirt color to complement or contrast with the design. Remember that pinkish letters might not show up well on a pinkish shirt-- if the two pinks are too alike.

Have something to "state" to the world. An effective message states it in a memorable way. Think about slogans that have survived the ages, easy word combinations that most everybody has heard. As the tee shirt designer, it's your job to produce new slogans, adages or attention-getting phrases. Short is commonly better as it's more easily remembered. But, even a longer message may be memorable if it flows and has rhythm or rhyme.

Try out different fonts. When picking out a font, remember that legibility counts. But so does visual aspect. Pick a font that adds a layer of depth to your message. If the message is, for instance, "Work drives me mad," then the font may be scribbled or crazy-looking, and yet still legible. Ideally, you'll make your design in a graphics program (like Photoshop) and then use your image atone of the sites.

Consider the art. Draw/design the art to express feelings. Which emotion do you want to conjure up? Distinguish the elements in the image that naturally arouse the desired response and then accent those elements. Are you seeking to make a sense of beauty or fright in those who see your design? The key is to comprehend the pieces of the artwork and build on them.

Place the art and text so that one doesn't distract from the other. Art may be behind the text--if the art itself isn't too busy. Art may be above or below the text. This works particularly well with oblong-shaped art so that the art basically underlines or sits above the line of text. Your art may also run along the side of the tee shirt, even crossing from front to back.

Scan and import your art images onto your file if you're using Photoshop or a like application. Incorporating art may enhance your message. Or utilize art by itself if the visual is the message you want to convey.

Chapter 4:

Produce a "Paper" and Sell Ads

Synopsis

This is a little more challenging, but once applied, may really draw you a whole gob of buyers! Here likewise, I'd target a professional market.

Ads

An illustration: In my city, there's a really prominent land agent. In all my years I had never seen this specific mode of advertising by an agent. He produced a "paper" about his geographic region. It's only five or six pages (11x17) and published on newspaper stock. It has all of the local activities, what's being constructed, how it will affect the biotic community, and so forth. Naturally, the paper is angled toward real estate news, but has just enough of the additional factors to draw in a loyal resident readership. In this paper, he deals ads to mortgage brokers, movers, title and loan companies, auto dealerships, and so forth. Now, when individuals go to sell their homes, who do you believe they're going to call? Him, naturally! Because his name is before them bringing them news pertinent to their day-to-day lives week in and week out.

It's crucial for you to know everything about your paper. If you're brand new and are making cold calls, you'll be pelted with questions about your publication. If you are able to answer them right, you'll build credibility with your prospects. If you blunder and can't give solid info, you'll struggle miserably.

You must be acquainted with your rates and the size of each ad you have for sale. Ads can be sold either by the column-inch or by the pages, which are subdivided into particular sizes like Full-page, Half-page, 1/4-page, and so forth. It's crucial that you become fully-able to spot an ad and distinguish its size. Charge this information to memory.

Make a list of the business people you know. Begin making calls to set up sales. If you're new to the ad sales game, it's safe to assume that you won't have an existing book of business. That surely doesn't mean that you won't be able to begin selling. Almost everybody knows somebody who's either in management or owns a business. This is your quick market.

It's important for you to produce a sense of urgency for your prospects. Don't be pushy, though. Nobody likes to be pressured into anything. But, keep in mind that you're not selling a physical product like a car or copy machine. Your job is to sell the "concept" of advertising.

Sell from the top down. This step is exceedingly important. Regardless of your prospect's budget, show them your biggest and most expensive ad first. They might only be thinking of a small ad, however, they might not comprehend that by spending a little more money, they'll be using their ad dollars more wisely.

Become a master at follow through. You'll find, after your first couple of months, that the bulk of your sales will happen as a result of follow up. Even seasoned pros don't make sales during first attempts. You should do a follow-up no later than 3 to 5 days after your first contact. After eight or ten unsuccessful tries to close a prospect, move on to another buyer. Your time is too valuable to waste on those who are not ready to purchase.

Chapter 5:

Write Resumes

Synopsis

All right, it's not glamorous. However, it may be lucrative and it's a never ending need. The fantastic thing about writing resumes is that it's an easy part of your business to develop and outsource if you don't like to do it, or don't have the time to commit to it.

For Others

At an ultra- low price of fifty dollars (I've been cited rates of $250 just for a resume); doing only a couple a day may add up to a very nice full-time income. Up-selling a package (e.g., cover letter and reference sheet) was commonly super easy, and customers were so thankful that this feeling alone was enough to make it worthwhile.

The hardest thing about writing a resume is knowing what to accent. You must attract the attention of HR managers, who receive 100s of resumes daily even when they haven't advertised any positions.

Write a cover letter. This isn't a synopsis of your resume. Merely introduce yourself and state why you're the best candidate for the job.

Know what type of job is being applied for and what the qualifications are for employment.

Pick a design for the resume. You are able to search for samples that are particular to the job being applied for, although it's more crucial to have an outline that best suits the job and fill in the blanks with the personal information. The outline may include objective, work experience, qualifications and references.

Put in the resume the objective, fitting the job description. This may determine whether the person gets the 10 to 30 second review and if the reviewer will send your resume to the next round.

Utilize bullet points to convey info and strive to be clear and concise when writing the rest of the resume. Analyze the job qualifications and spotlight any skills that meet those requirements. It's also best to utilize action words like prepared, directed, managed, developed, supervised, implemented, coordinated and awarded. If there is a lack of experience, center on how education has prepared the person for the position for which they are applying.

Include symbols like %, $, and #. These symbols will save space, letting you include more information on the resume. A symbol like a dollar sign may also draw the HR manager's attention to a significant financial accomplishment. For instance, "directed and closed first year with two million in revenue" should be altered to "directed and closed first year with $2M in revenue."

Spotlight strong points by putting the most relevant points first where they may be viewed quickly. Remain positive and prevent negatives like reasons for leaving an employer and history gaps in employment. These may be discussed in person if necessary.

Chapter 6:

Proof/Edit Pupil Papers

Synopsis

A lot of individuals today are always on the go-trying to get here or there.

Help Students

Ahhh, endearing, broke, despairing educatees. A lot of them don't have the time or, quite honestly, the skill level, to edit their own work. And, they'll gladly pay somebody to do it.

This is among the easiest markets to target as all you have to do is get hold of the Student Affairs office and ask to post a notice on the student message board. Or, you may take out an ad in the college newspaper. As well, flyers posted around the campus works well.

Commonly, if a student utilizes you once, they will always return if they're satisfied with your services. The finest part about this group? They have loudmouths and they utilize them -- to tell other pupils about your services.

Students likewise need resumes, bibliographies and graduate school essays. There are a plethora of services you are able to provide them successfully. I can tell you from personal experience that they are a good paying lot and are exceedingly nice to work with -- because they're commonly desperate and are just happy to find somebody who may work within their deadlines (think, "I required this yesterday!").

I don't suggest outright writing papers for pupils. I think it is immoral. However, proofing, editing, suggestive revisions -- these are all services that I have supplied quite successfully in the past.

Chapter 7:

Arrange Screenplays

Synopsis

A different starved bunch -- the playwright, writer, author, and so forth. When these artists present their work to official agencies, producers, guilds, and so on, they must be arranged a particular way. Screenplays have one format, treatments* a different, manuscripts some other.

Format

There's a software system for all of this. As a full-service editorial firm, if you buy the suitable software, you are able to market to a particular group and establish yourself as a go-to service for that business.

I executed this for those who composed screenplays. I bought the software and took out an ad in an industry paper for artists (actors, professional dancers, musicians, and so on.). My first customer paid for the software package.

This was in 1992 and I think I paid about $200 for the software package. But, the beginning job I did for this type of customer netted me $300 (that I unquestionably recall!). The good thing about soliciting this type of customer is that they forever need revisal, updates, extra copies, and so on. I had a fee for all of this, naturally.

I always told customers that I'd store the latest version of their work for them free of charge. This made them feel truly secure and thankful. How come? I discovered many creative persons to be forgetful and a little unorganized. By volunteering this "free of charge" service, they knew that if ever they couldn't find the latest version or their computer went down, that all they had to do was telephone me.

This reinforced client loyalty -- and led to immeasurable sums of business over the years. The amusing part about working with creative persons is that you get to view the creative procedure in motion.

I had 2 customers who processed the same screenplay for over 3 years. They must have paid me a couple of thousand dollars over this time as they made alterations, sent copies to different offices, and so forth.

*Treatments: Treatments are one-page summaries of scripts passed on to studios for consideration. Oftentimes, a creative person will submit a treatment. If the studio likes the treatment, they'll petition the full (or a partial) script.

The rationality behind treatments? Easy... time. Studios are deluged and they simply can't read through everything presented. This technique gives them an estimation of what a script is about without having to plod through the entire thing. So, basically, what studios purchase is a "theme", not a full-fledged script. This is likewise why what the writer envisioned is often not what it ends up to be.

Chapter 8:

Author A Hot Theme & Sell It

Synopsis

Daily news references (e.g., papers, news sites, and so on. are always seeking timely, well-written material) -- and, they'll commonly pay for them -- if they're soundly researched and you provide them exclusives to the piece.

Hot Topics

This will fly in the face of established soundness, but it's worked great for me for a long time. Rather than sending off a question, write a piece (e.g., mortgage fraudulence and its burden on the economy, and so forth.), research it well and propose it to daily news businesses.

I'd send the composition to no more than one place at a time and give them a deadline by which to reply. Let them know that as it's a time-sensitive composition, you'll give them "x" amount of time to reply (I commonly proposed three days) before proposing it to another business.

Sooner or later, somebody will pick the piece up if you abide by the method below.

Choose a hot topic: view the news and see what stories are creating every headline. For instance, hurricane season has arrived and the anniversary of Katrina just took place. Consider an issue around hurricanes and/or hurricane season and give it different angle (the outcomes of hurricanes for youngsters under twelve, and so on.).

Research exhaustively: Whatever subject you choose, make certain you reference two - four long-familiar sources. For instance, if you were going to author about hurricanes phone the National Weather Service and get a citation from an official there. Official news sources don't like to utilize unreferenced content; they prefer to state, "According to Tony Jones the head meteorologist at the National Weather Service, . . ."

Aim for daily news providers: every day news sources are the ones who are most likely to choose this type of material because they're perpetually under the gun to keep the news recent.

Wrapping Up

A final thought...

Phone old customers. It's an old business axiom that eighty percent of your business will come from twenty percent of your customers. So, phone your usuals. Ask them if they've anything or if they may refer you to somebody who may need your services.

I've discovered that the best way do this is to up-sell something. For instance, if you just completed a sales letter for a customer, ask them if they require a brochure, post card or e-zine to supplement that. Pros recognize that advertising and marketing isn't a one-hit marvel. So, many are hospitable to utilizing more than one technique to reach customers.

As a matter of fact, many utilize one technique to reach customers (e.g., a sales letter), and some other to stay in touch (for instance, a weekly e-zine). But, it might not occur to them to apply these procedures thru one provider (you!).

So, it's up to you to make them recognize the value you furnish. And, by thinking proactively, you look ultra- sharp, professional and forward-thinking - which only means more work for you!